Stage 3 Pack A

Floppy's Phonics Fiction

Kate Ruttle

C ng Notes

Contents

Introduction 2
Phonic focus 3
Vocabulary 4
Comprehension strategies 5
Curriculum coverage charts 6

Leek Hotpot

Guided or group reading 10
Group and independent reading activities 11
Speaking, listening and drama activities 12
Writing activities 13

Queen's Maid

Guided or group reading 14
Group and independent reading activities 15
Speaking, listening and drama activities 16
Writing activities 17

Toads in the Road

Guided or group reading 18
Group and independent reading activities 19
Speaking, listening and drama activities 20
Writing activities 21

Chairs in the Air

Guided or group reading 22
Group and independent reading activities 23
Speaking, listening and drama activities 24
Writing activities 25

A Bark in the Night

Guided or group reading 26
Group and independent reading activities 27
Speaking, listening and drama activities 28
Writing activities 28

Silver Foil Rocket

Group or guided reading 29
Group and independent reading activities 30
Speaking, listening and drama activities 31
Writing activities 32

Introduction

Welcome to *Floppy's Phonics!* This series gives you decodable phonic stories featuring all your favourite *Oxford Reading Tree* characters. The books provide the perfect opportunity for consolidation and practice of synthetic phonics within a familiar setting, to build your children's confidence. As well as having a strong phonic focus, each story is a truly satisfying read with lots of opportunities for comprehension, so they are fully in line with the simple view of reading.

Phonic development

The *Floppy's Phonics* Stage 3 stories support a synthetic phonics approach to early reading skills and are closely aligned to *Letters and Sounds*. They should be used for practice and consolidation. The books should be read in the suggested order (see chart on page 3), so that children can benefit from the controlled introduction, revision and consolidation of the phonemes. They can be read before the *Floppy's Phonics Non-fiction* books at the same stage. In addition, they can be used for practice and consolidation after introducing the sounds with other programmes.

The series can be used by children working within Phase 3 of *Letters and Sounds*, to support children as they broaden their knowledge of graphemes and phonemes for use in reading and spelling. The books will help to embed these vital early phonics skills, and help to ensure that children will experience success in learning to read and thus will be motivated to keep on reading.

Your children will benefit most from reading *Floppy's Phonics Stage 3* if they are able to:

- recognize the vowel digraphs from *Letters and Sounds* Phase 3
- blend and segment CVC words, including vowel and consonant digraphs (e.g. *shop*)
- recognize the *Letters and Sounds* high frequency words for Phase 3

Phonic focus

This chart shows which phonemes are introduced and practised in each title.

Title	ORT Stage Book band colour Year group	*Letters and Sounds* phase	Phonemes introduced	Phonemes revisited
Leek Hotpot	Stage 3 Yellow Year 1 / P2	Phase Three	ee oo (short)	ch th sh
The Queen's Maid	Stage 3 Yellow Year 1 / P2	Phase Three	ai ow	ee ch ng sh qu ll
Toads in the Road	Stage 3 Yellow Year 1 / P2	Phase Three	oa ur	sh ch qu ng ow ck
Chairs in the Air	Stage 3 Yellow Year 1 / P2	Phase Three	air ear or	ow ur ee oo (short) ng sh ch ck
A Bark in the Night	Stage 3 Yellow Year 1 / P2	Phase Three	ar er igh oo (long)	ear ee oa ow
Silver Foil Rocket	Stage 3 Yellow Year 1 / P2	Phase Three	oi ure	or er ar ow oo ee

Vocabulary

Most of the common words introduced in *Floppy's Phonics* are phonically decodable, using phonic skills and knowledge that are gradually developed through the stories. *Floppy's Phonics* also introduces the high frequency words which are listed in *Letters and Sounds.* High frequency words are common words which occur frequently in children's books. Many of them are decodable, some of them are 'tricky'. The words are defined in line with *Letters and Sounds*.

High frequency (HF) decodable words

Many of the high frequency words are decodable by saying and blending the sounds, and children should practise them regularly so that they can read them automatically as soon as possible.

High frequency (HF) tricky words

Some of the high frequency words are 'tricky', that is, they contain unusual grapheme-phoneme correspondences (e.g. *we, they*). The advice in *Letters and Sounds* is that children should be taught to recognize the phonemes they know within these words and to distinguish these from the tricky bits. For example, in the word *they,* children should be taught to recognize the grapheme *th* and then taught the tricky sound of 'ey' in this context.

Context words

In most of the books in *Floppy's Phonics* there are one or two other words, including the characters' names, which cannot be read using phonics alone, but which add to the child's enjoyment and understanding of the story. These words are listed as 'context words'.

The characters in these books are Mum, Dad, Biff, Chip, Kipper, Gran and Floppy. The names of the characters are listed as context words if they are not yet decodable.

The table on page 5 shows the context words, and the Phase 3 high frequency decodable and tricky words which appear in each story.

High frequency words used in each book

Leek Hotpot	HF decodable words	will this with look(s) for then them see
	HF tricky words	they we you me all
	Context words	Floppy
The Queen's Maid	HF decodable words	will down that now
	HF tricky words	my was her all me be you are
	Context words	Wilf
Toads in the Road	HF decodable words	for will now
	HF tricky words	you they are was we
	Context words	–
Chairs in the Air	HF decodable words	them with now down look too that for
	HF tricky words	me, was, has
	Context words	Wilf
A Bark in the Night	HF decodable words	they then too with
	HF tricky words	was he you
	Context words	Floppy
Silver Foil Rocket	HF decodable words	for them
	HF tricky words	was they we be you no that
	Context words	–

Comprehension Strategies

Reading is about making meaning, and it is particularly important that a child's earliest reading books offer opportunities for making meaning and telling a complete story. As with all *Oxford Reading Tree* stories, the titles in *Floppy's Phonics* are fun stories which children will really enjoy, and which will give you lots of scope for practising and extending their comprehension skills.

Story	Comprehension strategy taught through these Group/Guided Reading Notes				
	Prediction	Questioning	Clarifying	Summarising	Imagining
Leek Hotpot	✓		✓		✓
The Queen's Maid	✓	✓	✓	✓	✓
Toads in the Road	✓		✓	✓	✓
Chairs in the Air	✓	✓	✓		✓
A Bark in the Night	✓	✓	✓	✓	✓
Silver Foil Rocket	✓		✓	✓	

Curriculum coverage charts

Key

C = Language comprehension   Y = Year   P = Primary

W = Word recognition

In the designations such as 5.2, the first number represents the strand and the second number the individual objective

	Speaking, Listening, Drama	Reading	Writing
Leek Hotpot			
PNS Literacy Framework (Y1)	1.1, 1.2, 2.1 3.1 4.1	W 5.1, 5.2, 5.4 C 6.5, 7.1	10.1
National Curriculum	working within level 1		
Scotland (5–14) (P2)	CfE First Level 5-14 Level A Listening for Information Listening in Groups Responding to Texts Talking in Groups Talking about texts	CfE First Level 5-14 Level A Reading for Information Reading for enjoyment Reading to reflect on craft Read aloud	CfE First Level 5-14 Level A Functional writing Personal writing Imaginative writing Punctuation and Structure Spelling Handwriting
N. Ireland (P2)	1, 2, 3, 6, 8, 10, 11	1, 2, 3, 4	1, 3
Wales Key Stage 1	Range: 1, 3, 4 Skills: 2, 3, 4, 5 Lang Dev: 3	Range: 1, 2, 4, 5, 6 Skills: 1, 2 Lang Dev: 1, 2	Range: 2, 3, 4 Skills: 1, 2, 3, 4, 6, 7, 8, 9 Lang Dev: 1, 4
Queen's Maid			
PNS Literacy Framework (Y1)	1.1 2.1 3.1 4.1	W 5.1, 5.2, 5.3, 5.5 C 8.2	11.1
National Curriculum	Working towards level 1		

Curriculum coverage charts

	Speaking, Listening, Drama	Reading	Writing
Scotland (5–14) (P1)	CfE First Level 5-14 Level A Listening for Information Listening in Groups Responding to Texts Talking in Groups Talking about Texts	CfE First Level 5-14 Level A Reading for Information Reading for enjoyment Reading to reflect on craft Read aloud	CfE First Level 5-14 Level A Functional writing Personal writing Imaginative writing Punctuation and Structure Spelling Handwriting
N. Ireland (P1)	1, 2, 3, 6, 8, 10, 11	1, 2, 3, 4	1, 3
Wales Key Stage 1	Range: 1, 3, 5 Skills: 2, 3, 4, 5, 6 Lang Dev: 3	Range: 1, 2, 4, 5, 6 Skills: 1, 2 Lang Dev: 1, 2	Range: 2, 3, 4 Skills: 1, 2, 3, 4, 6, 7, 8, 9 Lang Dev: 1, 4
Toads in the Road			
PNS Literacy Framework (Y1)	1.1, 1.2 2.1 3.1 4.1	W 5.1, 5.2, 5.5 C 6.1, 6.2	10.1
National Curriculum	Working within level 1		
Scotland (5–14) (P1)	CfE First Level 5-14 Level A Listening for Information Listening in Groups Responding to Texts Talking in Groups Talking about Texts	LCfE First Level 5-14 Level A Reading for Information Reading for enjoyment Reading to reflect on craft Read aloud	CfE First Level 5-14 Level A Functional writing Personal writing Imaginative writing Punctuation and Structure Spelling Handwriting
N. Ireland (P1)	1, 2, 3, 6, 8, 10, 11	1, 2, 3, 4	1, 3
Wales Key Stage 1	Range: 1, 3, 5 Skills: 2, 3, 4, 5, 6 Lang Dev: 3	Range: 1, 2, 4, 5, 6 Skills: 1, 2 Lang Dev: 1, 2	Range: 2, 3, 4 Skills: 1, 2, 3, 4, 6, 7, 8, 9 Lang Dev: 1, 4

Curriculum coverage charts

	Speaking, Listening, Drama	Reading	Writing
Chairs in the Air			
PNS Literacy Framework (Y1)	1.1 2.1 3.1, 3.XX 4.1	W 5.1, 5.5 C 6.1, 8.2	12.3
National Curriculum	Working within level 1		
Scotland (5–14) (P1)	CfE First Level 5-14 Level A Listening for Information Listening in Groups Responding to Texts Talking in Groups Talking about texts	CfE First Level 5-14 Level A Reading for Information reading for enjoyment reading to reflect on craft Read aloud	CfE First Level 5-14 Level A Functional writing Personal writing Imaginative writing Punctuation and Structure Spelling Handwriting
N. Ireland (P1)	1, 2, 3, 6, 8, 10, 11	1, 2, 3, 4	1, 3
Wales Key Stage 1	Range: 1, 3, Skills: 2, 3, 4, 5, 6 Lang Dev: 3	Range: 1, 2, 4, 5, 6 Skills: 1, 2, 3 Lang Dev: 1, 2	Range: 2, 3, 4 Skills: 1, 2, 3, 4, 6, 7, 8, 9 Lang Dev: 1, 4
A Bark in the Night			
PNS Literacy Framework (Y1)	1.1 2.1 3.1 4.1, 4.2	W 5.1, 5.7 C 6.2, 8.2	11.1
National Curriculum	Working within level 1		
Scotland (5–14) (P1)	CfE First Level 5-14 Level A Listening for Information Listening in Groups Responding to Texts Talking in Groups Talking about texts	CfE First Level 5-14 Level A Reading for Information Reading for enjoyment Reading to reflect on craft Read aloud	CfE First Level 5-14 Level A Functional writing Personal writing Imaginative writing Punctuation and Structure Spelling Handwriting

Curriculum coverage charts

	Speaking, Listening, Drama	Reading	Writing
N. Ireland (P1)	1, 2, 3, 6, 8, 10, 11	1, 2, 3, 4	1, 3
Wales Key Stage 1	Range: 1, 3, 5 Skills: 2, 3, 4, 5, 6 Lang Dev: 3	Range: 1, 2, 4, 5, 6 Skills: 1, 2 Lang Dev: 1, 2	Range: 2, 3, 4 Skills: 1, 2, 3, 4, 6, 7, 8, 9 Lang Dev: 1, 4
Silver Foil Rocket			
PNS Literacy Framework (Y1)	1.1 2.1, 2.2 3.1 4.1	W 5.1, 5.2, 5.7 C 6.2, 7.3	9.3
National Curriculum	Working within level 1		
Scotland (5–14) (P1)	CfE First Level 5-14 Level A Listening for Information Listening in Groups Responding to Texts Talking in Groups Talking about Texts	CfE First Level 5-14 Level A Reading for Information Reading for enjoyment Reading to reflect on craft Read aloud	CfE First Level 5-14 Level A Functional writing Personal writing Imaginative writing Punctuation and Structure Spelling Handwriting
N. Ireland (P1)	1, 2, 3, 6, 8, 10, 11	1, 2, 3, 4	1, 3
Wales Key Stage 1	Range: 1, 3, 4 Skills: 2, 3, 4, 5 Lang Dev: 3	Range: 1, 2, 4, 5, 6 Skills: 1, 2 Lang Dev: 1, 2	Range: 2 Skills: 1, 2, 3, 4, 6, 7, 8, 9 Lang Dev: 1

Leek Hotpot

C = Language comprehension   W = Word recognition

Phonic Focus:

Phonemes introduced in this book: ee, oo (short)
Phonemes revisited include: ch, th, ck
Context word: Floppy

Guided or group reading

Introducing the book

W Can children read the title? Remind them what makes the sound /ee/.

- Do they remember the strategy of looking for letters that don't usually go together to find the place where syllables meet? (tp)
- Read the title together : L–ee–k H–o–t–p–o–t

W Turn to page 1 and show the children the word *cookbook.* Find the syllable boundary (kb). Introduce the phoneme of short /oo/ and read the word: c–oo–k–b–oo–k.

C *(Predicting)* Encourage children to use prediction: *What do you think the children will make for Mum?*

- Look through the book, talking about what happens on each page. Use some of the high frequency words as you discuss the story (see chart on page 5).

Strategy check

Remind children to sound the words out carefully, remembering that sometimes two letters can represent one sound. If they can't sound out a word, do they already know it from memory?

Independent reading

- Ask children to read the story aloud. Praise and encourage them while they read, and prompt as necessary.

C *(Clarifying)* Ask children to explain where Mum was for most of this story.

Assessment Check that children:

- *(AF 1)* use phonic knowledge to sound out and blend the phonemes in words (see chart on page 5)
- *(AF 2)* use comprehension skills to work out what is happening
- *(AF 1)* make a note of any difficulties the children encounter and of strategies they use to solve problems.

Returning to the text

W Can children find words with *oo* in them? How about *ee*? Which list is longer?

Assessment *(AF 1)* Discuss any words the children found tricky and talk about strategies used.

Group and independent reading activities

Objective recognize alternative ways of spelling phonemes (5.2).

W **You will need:** flashcards showing the words: *book, cook, look, took, shook, foot, good, wood, wool.*

- Show children the word *look.* Ask them to draw sound buttons to show which letters represent which sound.
- Show all of the flashcards, asking children to sound out and read the words.
- Which consonants can children find at the end of these words? (k, t, d, l*).* Which one is most common? (k)
- Explain that short *oo* is only followed by these consonants, most commonly by *k.*

Assessment *(AF 1)* Can children read the words and count the phonemes?

Objective Recognize automatically an increasing number of high frequency words (5.4).

W **You will need:** two copies each of the flashcards: *will, this, with, see, they, we, you, then, look.* Add any previously taught high frequency words which are not yet securely learned.

- Shuffle the cards and line the children up. Show the top card to the first child. If they read the card successfully, they go to the end of the line and you put the card down. If they make an error, they go to the end of the line and you show the same card to the next child.
- Time the children to see how quickly they get through the whole pile of cards twice.
- Repeat. Can the children knock seconds off their time?

Assessment *(AF 1)* Can children read the words automatically?

Objective To read and spell phonically decodable two syllable words (6.5).

W Check children's understanding of the word 'syllable'. Clarify that it means a 'beat' in a word. Count how many syllables there are in *Hotpot, Floppy, Biff, Chip, cookbook.*

- Show the children the words *cookbook* and *hotpot.* Explain that these compound words have each been made up of two smaller words. Can children identify the two short words each time?
- Show other compound words like: *cobweb, eggshell, pigtail, cowshed.*
- Show children the word 'notpot'. This isn't a real word. Talk about why the author wrote it and how readers can read it.

Assessment *(AF 1)* Can the children read and spell the two syllable compound words?

Objective Identify the main events and characters in stories (7.1).

C *(Clarifying)*

- Ask children who they think the main characters are in this story.
- List the characters.
- Can the children rank them in importance?
- Revisit the book to help the children to discuss the importance to the storyline of Floppy, Biff, Chip, Kipper, Mum and Dad.

Assessment *(AF 4)* Can the children justify their ideas about the characters' importance?

Speaking, listening and drama activities

Objective Order events using story language (1.2).

C *(Imagining)*

- Re-read the book, asking children to put their hands up when they are finding out something about cooking leek hotpot.
- Gather small world toys – or pictures from the internet – to represent each of the necessary things: leeks, chicken, deep pot, hob.
- Ask children to 'think–pair–share' with a partner to explain the sequence of events.

Assessment *(AF 4)* Can the children order the events appropriately?

Writing activities

Objective Write a chronological text using simple structures (10.1).

C *(Clarifying)*

- Revisit the steps needed to make Leek Hotpot.
- Show children the cookbook that Biff is holding on page 6.
- Ask them to write the recipe that Biff is following.

Assessment *(Writing AF 3)* Can the children sequence the steps in their recipe?

Queen's Maid

C = Language comprehension W = Word recognition

Phonic Focus:

Phonemes introduced in this book: ai, ow

Phonemes revisited include: ee, ll, ch, ng, sh, qu

Context word: Wilf

Guided or group reading

Introducing the book

W Can children read the title? Explain that the two letters *ai* join together to make the sound /ai/ and that *ee* makes the sound /ee/. Read the title together : Qu–ee–n–s M–ai–d

W Turn to page 1 and show the children *ow.* Explain that *ow* represents the long vowel sound /ow/.

C *(Predicting)* Encourage children to use prediction: *Who do you think the Queen is in this story? Who is her maid?*

- Look through the book, talking about what happens on each page. Use some of the high frequency words as you discuss the story (see chart on page 5).

Strategy check

Remind the children to sound the words out carefully, remembering that sometimes two letters can represent one sound. If they can't sound out a word, do they already know it from memory?

Independent reading

- Ask children to read the story aloud. Praise and encourage them while they read, and prompt as necessary.

C *(Clarifying)* Ask children to explain where Wilma met Queen Hatpin.

Assessment Check that children:

- *(AF 1)* use phonic knowledge to sound out and blend the phonemes in words (see chart on page 3).
- *(AF 2)* use comprehension skills to work out what is happening.
- *(AF 1)* make a note of any difficulties the children encounter and of strategies they use to solve problems.

Returning to the text

W Can children find words with *ow* in them? How about *ai*? Which list is longer?

Assessment *(AF 1)* Discuss any words the children found tricky and talk about strategies used.

Group and independent reading activities

Objective Recognize phonemes (5.2).

W **You will need:** plastic letter and digraphs : *ow, ai, ee, sh, qu, n, p, w, t, d.*

- Place *ow* on the table and ask children if they remember the long vowel phoneme. Say it together. Repeat for *ai* and *ee.*
- Make the word *queen*. Say it together and count the phonemes (3). Check that children recognize which phonemes are represented by which letters.
- Repeat for other words e.g.: *pain, wait, down.*

Assessment *(AF 1)* Can children read the words and count the phonemes?

Objective Apply phonic knowledge and skills to reading unfamiliar words (5.5).

W Make the word *maid.* Ask children to read it.

- Draw sound buttons to match the letters to the phonemes.
- Change the *m* for a *p*. Can children read the new word?
- Can they show you how to change *paid* into *pain* then *pail, wail, wait*?

Assessment *(AF 1)* Can children read the words each time and tell you how to make the next word?

Objective To identify the constituent parts of two syllable words (5.3).

W Check children's understanding of the word 'syllable'. Clarify that it means a 'beat' in a word. Count how many syllables there are in *Wilma, Wilf, Mum, Queen, Hatpin*. How many syllables are in your children's names?

- Ask children to find the queen's name in the book: *Hatpin.*
- Can they explain how they read it?
- Introduce the strategy of finding the letters that don't go together (tp) and recognizing that this must be where syllables join.
- Read the syllables separately.

Assessment *(AF 1)* Can the children find the syllable boundaries in other two syllable words, e.g. in their names?

Objective To visualize and comment on characters, making links to own experiences (8.2).

C *(Questioning)*

- Clarify that Wilma met Queen Hatpin in a dream.
- Think questions to ask Wilma about her dream. The questions could relate to Wilma or to Queen Hatpin.
- Encourage questions about feelings and motivation as well as events.

Assessment *(AF 2 and 3)* Can the children think of appropriate questions to ask Wlima?

Speaking, listening and drama activities

Objective Explore familiar themes and characters through improvisation and role play (4.1).

C *(Imagining)*

- Give each of the children a brief opportunity to be hot–seated as one of the characters in the story. They could be Wilma, Wilf, Mum or Queen Hatpin.
- Before each hot–seating session, let the questioners have some time to develop their questions while the hot–seated child tries to learn more about the character from the book.

Assessment *(AF 2 and 3)* Can the children use the text and their imaginations to ask and answer questions appropriately?

Writing activities

Objective Compose and write simple sentences independently to communicate meaning (11.1).

C *(Summarising)*

- Ask children to think about the events in the story. What were the important things that happened?
- Give children a sheet with either three or four boxes. In each box, ask children to write a sentence explaining one of the important things that happened in the story.
- After they have written their ideas, let the children compare and comment on each others' ideas.
- They should then order their ideas so that they fit the chronology of the story.

Toads in the Road

C = Language comprehension   W = Word recognition

Phonic Focus:

Phonemes introduced in this book: oa, ur
Phonemes revisited include: sh, ch, ck, qu, ng, ow

Guided or group reading

Introducing the book

- W Can children read the title? Tell them that the two letters *oa* join together to make the sound /oa/. Read: *T–oa–d–s in the R–oa–d*
- W Turn to pages 1–2. How many *oa* words can the children read?
- Introduce *ur* in *hurt.* Can the children sound out the word: *h–ur–t* and draw sound buttons?
- C *(Predicting)* Encourage children to use prediction: What can everyone do to help the toads?
- Look through the book, talking about what happens on each page. Use some of the high frequency words as you discuss the story (see chart on page 5).

Strategy check

Remind the children to sound the words out carefully, remembering that sometimes two letters can represent one sound. If they can't sound out a word, do they already know it from memory?

Independent reading

- Ask children to read the story aloud. Praise and encourage them while they read, and prompt as necessary.
- C *(Clarifying)* Ask children to explain how the toads are kept safe in the end.

Assessment Check that children:

- *(AF 1)* use phonic knowledge to sound out and blend the phonemes in words (see chart on page 5).
- *(AF 2)* use comprehension skills to work out what is happening.
- *(AF 1)* make a note of any difficulties the children encounter and of strategies they use to solve problems.

Returning to the text

W Could children read the word *under*? Which bit was tricky?

Assessment *(AF 1)* Discuss any words the children found tricky and talk about strategies used.

Group and independent reading activities

Objective *(6.2)* Segment words into their constituent phonemes in order to spell them correctly.

W Write the letters c___t. Say the word *coat.* How many phonemes are there? (3) Can the children work out which sound is missing? Do they remember which letters are used to show the sound?

- Ask them to write the word.
- Repeat for *r__d, c__t, c__ch.*
- Do the same for *h__t, t__n, b__n.*

Assessment *(AF 1)* Can children spell all the words?

Objective Recognize phonemes (5.2).

W **You will need:** two copies of flashcards for: *road, toad, coal, goal, coat, goat, oak, soak; turn, burn.*

- Hold up the cards, one at a time and check that all of the children can read the words.
- Mix the flashcards, face down and distribute them amongst the children.
- Play rhyming Snap!

Assessment *(AF 1)* Can children read the words and recognize the rhyming paris?

Objective Apply phonic knowledge and skill (5.5).

W Read the text on pages 2–3. Focus on the words: *croak* and *pond.*

- Ask children to draw sound buttons under *c–r–oa–k* and *p–o–n–d.*
- Ask children to count the number of letters and sounds in each of the words.
- Can they blend the phonemes to read the words?

Assessment Can children blend the adjacent consonants to read the words?

Objective Visualise and comment on events, making links to own experiences. Use phonic knowledge to write simple regular words (6.1).

C *(Imagining)*

- Look at the last picture together. How are the toads managing to get safely to the pond now?
- Look back through the book to find how the toad road was installed.
- Ask children to talk about this as a solution to the problem.
- Have they seen toad roads? How about support for other creatures to keep safe? Perhaps they might have seen notices to alert people to ducks crossing, to deer or racehorses horses crossing the road.
- Make links to school crossing patrols and other safety signs children might have seen.

Assessment *(AF 1)* Can children blend the phonemes for reading as well as segment them for spelling?

Speaking, listening and drama activities

Objective Retell stories, ordering events using story language.

C *(Summarising)*

- Use small world resources to re–enact the story.
- Ask children to assemble everything they need. If they don't have enough toads, what else could they use?

- Let one child narrate the story from the point of view of Dad, while others mime the events.
- Let children take turns at being the narrator.

Assessment *(AF 3)* Can children relate the events in the right order?

Writing activities

Objective Writes chronological texts using simple structures (10.1).

C *(Summarising)*

- Ask children to retell the story using pictures and events in the book.
- Remind them to use capital letters and full stops in their sentences.

Assessment *(Writing AF 6)* Can children retell the story successfully?

Chairs in the Air

C = Language comprehension **W** = Word recognition

Phonic Focus:

Phonemes introduced in this book: air, ear, or
Phonemes revisited include: sh, ch, ck, ck, ow, ur, ee, oo (short), ng
Context word: Wilf

Guided or group reading

Introducing the book

- **W** Can children read the title? Explain that the three letters *air* join together to make the sound /air/. Read the title together : Ch–air–s in the Air
- **W** Turn to page 1 and show the children *hear.* Explain that *ear* represents the long vowel sound /ear/.
- **C** *(Predicting)* Encourage children to use prediction: *What do you think Chairs in the Air is going to be?*
- Look through the book, talking about what happens on each page. Use some of the high frequency words as you discuss the story (see chart on page 5).

Strategy check

Remind the children to sound the words out carefully, remembering that sometimes two letters can represent one sound. If they can't sound out a word, do they already know it from memory?

Independent reading

- Ask children to read the story aloud. Praise and encourage them while they read, and prompt as necessary.
- **C** *(Clarifying)* Ask children to explain where Pompom ran off to.

Assessment Check that the children:

- *(AF 1)* use phonic knowledge to sound out and blend the phonemes in words (see chart on page 3).

- *(AF 2)* use comprehension skills to work out what is happening.
- *(AF 1)* make a note of any difficulties the children encounter and of strategies they use to solve problems.

Returning to the text

W Can children find words with *ear* in them? How about *air*? Which list is longer?

Assessment *(AF 1)* Discuss any words the children found tricky and talk about strategies used.

Group and independent reading activities

Objective Spell new words using phonics as the prime approach (6.1).

W Ask children to write *air* and *ear* on their whiteboards.

- Tell them that you are going to tell them a word beginning and they have to decide whether to make an *air* words or an *ear* words.
- Offer beginnings: *h, ch, g, n, t, y, f, p.*
- Discuss words the children make. If they make a word which is incorrectly spelled (e.g. *chear* instead of *cheer*) , show them the correct spelling, whist congratulating them for the thinking.

Assessment *(AF 1)* Can children make good decisions and spell the words appropriately?

Objective To apply phonic knowledge and skills as the prime approach to reading unfamiliar words (5.5).

W Revisit page 2. Read the text together, including the environmental print. Focus on the word *popcorn.*

- Ask children to draw sound buttons under what they know and to identify the 'tricky parts' of the word (*or*). Can they work out the whole word from what they do know?

Assessment *(AF 1)* Can the children identify the tricky bits in the word?

Objective Apply phonic knowledge and skills to reading unfamiliar words (5.5).

W Write the words *sick* and *stick.* Ask children to find what is the same and what is different between the words.

- Can they draw sound buttons to show the similarities and differences?
- Ask children to draw sound buttons and read *c–l–ear, s–p–ear, s–t–air.*

Assessment *(AF 1)* Can children use sound buttons to differentiate the adjacent consonants at the beginning of the words.

Objective To visualize and comment on characters, making links to own experiences (8.2).

C *(Questioning)*

- As a group, try to create a map of the fairground.
- The map should include all of the elements included in the book, but can also have any rides or stalls from fairs that the children have visited.

Assessment *(AF 2 and 3)* Can the children think of appropriate questions to ask Wlima?

Objective Make predictions showing an understanding of ideas, events and characters.

C *(Questioning)*

- Look for evidence of Pompom and her owner in the pictures and text throughout the book.
- What is Pompom's story?
- Talk about why Pompom might have run off each time.

Assessment *(AF3)* Can the children contribute reasons and suggestions about Pompom or her owner?

Speaking, listening and drama activities

Objective Take turns to speak, listen to others and talk about what they're going to do (3.1).

C *(Imagining)*

- As a group, try to create a map of the fairground.

- The map should include all of the elements included in the book, but can also have any rides or stalls from fairs that the children have visited.
- Once the map has been completed, use small world characters to show where Wilf and Chip went in the fairground.

Assessment *(AF 2)* Can the children use the text and their imaginations to make appropriate suggestions?

Writing activities

Objective Use the space bar and keyboard to type simple texts (12.3).

C *(Summarising)*

- Help children to find images of fairground rides on the internet.
- *(Writing AF 2)* They should label the rides, naming them if possible, and briefly explaining why these are or are not enjoyable rides.

A Bark in the Night

C = Language comprehension   W = Word recognition

Phonic Focus:

Phonemes introduced in this book: ar, igh, oo(long), er

Phonemes revisited include: ear, ee, oa, ow

Context word: Floppy

Guided or group reading

Introducing the book

W Can children read the title? Explain that the three letters *igh* join together to make the sound /igh/, and the *ar* shows /ar/. Read the title together : *A B–ar–k in the n–igh–t.*

W Turn to page 5 and show the children *soon.* Explain that the same letters *oo*, can represent the vowel sound in *look* as well as the vowel sound in *moon.*

C *(Predicting)* Encourage children to use prediction: *What do you think might happen in the night?*

- Look through the book, talking about what happens on each page. Use some of the high frequency words as you discuss the story (see chart on page 5).

Strategy check

Remind the children to sound the words out carefully, remembering that sometimes two letters can represent one sound. If they can't sound out a word, do they already know it from memory?

Independent reading

- Ask children to read the story aloud. Praise and encourage them while they read, and prompt as necessary.

C *(Clarifying)* Ask children to talk about how Dad felt when Kipper woke him up.

Assessment Check that children:

- *(AF 1)* use phonic knowledge to sound out and blend the phonemes in words (see chart on page 3).

- *(AF 2)* use comprehension skills to work out what is happening.
- *(AF 1)* note any difficulties the children encounter and of strategies used.

Returning to the text

W Can children find words with *igh* in them? How about *ar*? Which list is longer?

Assessment *(AF 1)* Discuss any words the children found tricky and talk about strategies used.

Group and independent reading activities

Objective Recognize alternative ways of pronouncing graphemes (5.1).

W **You will need:** flashcards with the words: *book, cook, look, good, foot, wood, wool, stood; food, boot, cool, loop, pool, moon, roof, spoon.*

- Put the words *look* and *moon* on the table.
- One at a time, introduce the other words and ask children to decide whether it is a long *oo* or short *oo* word.
- Teach children the strategy of trying both pronunciations if they're not sure.
- Ask children to read all of the words on both lists.

Assessment *(AF 1)* Can children make good decisions distributing the words appropriately?

Objective To segment words into the constituent phonemes in order to spell them correctly (6.2).

W Write the word *night.* Ask the children to draw sound buttons to show how the letters represent the sounds in the word.

- Now ask them to write *night.* Compare their version with yours.
- Ask them to write other *igh* words: *right, tight, fright, light, high, sigh.*

Assessment *(AF 1)* Can the children spell the *igh* words?

Objective Read phonically decodable two syllable words (5.7).

W Remind the children what 'syllable' means.

- Discuss ways of recognizing words with more than one syllable.
- Ask children to look for two syllable words in the text. These include: *camping, farmer, farmyard, harder, supper, Kipper, asleep, started, barking, midnight, lighter.*

- Talk about whether the ways they found of looking for words was good.
- Read all of the words together. Talk about strategies for reading them.

Assessment *(AF 1)* Can children identify and read the two syllable words?

Objective To comment on characters, making imaginative links to own experiences (8.2).

C *(Questioning)*

- As a group, consider questions that you would like to ask Dad.
- The questions could relate to events in or surrounding the book.
- Once questions have been framed, you could be the first to take the role of Dad in order to model possible answers to some of the questions. Encourage subsequent 'Dads' to think of different answers to some of the questions.

Assessment *(AF 2 and 3)* Can the children think of appropriate questions to ask of Dad?

Speaking, listening and drama activities

Objective Act out stories, using different voices for characters (4.2).

C *(Imagining)*

- In pairs, ask the children to role-play the events in the book.
- One of the two children should be Dad and the other should be Kipper, then the night creatures.
- Encourage the characters to have dialogue and discussion, perhaps informed by the hot–seating activity.

Assessment *(AF 2)* Can the children use the text and their imaginations to develop appropriate dialogue, using good voices?

Writing activities

Objective Compose and write simple sentences to communicate meaning (11.1).

C *(Summarising)*

- Ask children to draw a picture of Dad with a big speech bubble. In his speech bubble, he can tell Mum about his night on the farm.

Assessment *(Writing AF 2)* Can the children create an appropriate text, independently?

Silver Foil Rocket

C = Language comprehension | W = Word recognition

Phonic Focus:

Phonemes introduced in this book: oi, er, ure

Phonemes revisited include: ar, ow, oo, ee

Context word: Wilf

Guided or group reading

Introducing the book

W Can children read the title? Explain that the letters *oi* join together to make the sound /oi/. Read the title together: *S–i–l–v–er F–oi–l R–o–ck–e–t*

W Turn to page 3 and show the children *Spoil Sports.* Do they recognize the oi? Explain that *or* represents the /or/ sound as in sport.

C *(Predicting)* Encourage children to use prediction: *What do you think the children will go as?*

- Look through the book, talking about what happens on each page. Use some of the high frequency words as you discuss the story (see chart on page 5).

Strategy check

Remind the children to sound the words out carefully, remembering that sometimes two letters can represent one sound. If they can't sound out a word, do they already know it from memory?

Independent reading

- Ask children to read the story aloud. Praise and encourage them while they read, and prompt as necessary.

C *(Clarifying)* Ask children why it was Kipper who received the cup.

Assessment Check that children:

- *(AF 1)* use phonic knowledge to sound out and blend the phonemes in words (see chart on page 3).

- *(AF 2)* use comprehension skills to work out what is happening.
- *(AF 1)* make a note of any difficulties the children encounter and of strategies they use to solve problems.

Returning to the text

W Can children find words with *oi* in them? How about *or*? Which list is longer?

Assessment *(AF 1)* Discuss any words the children found tricky and talk about strategies used.

Group and independent reading activities

Objective Recognize ways of spelling phonemes (5.2).

W **You will need:** flashcards showing: ar, or, ur

- Show the children the flashcards and ensure that they know the graphemes.
- Write a word frame e.g. s____t. Ask the children to decide which of the three vowel digraphs can be written into the word frame to make a word. Model the strategy of trying them, one at a time, and saying aloud the word that you make.
- Repeat for other word frames e.g. p__t, h__t, f__k, sp__t, c__k, b__n, t__n, c__t, ch__ch, sc__f, st__t.

Assessment *(AF 1)* Can children read the words and non-words they make?

Objective To segment words into the constituent phonemes in order to spell them correctly (6.2).

W Draw a phoneme frame with four spaces.

- Say the word *foil.* Ask children to sound–talk the word to establish the number of phonemes, then to represent each phoneme with letters in the phoneme frame.
- Can children find the word in the book to compare your spelling with?
- Use the phoneme frame to spell the words: *coin, join, soil* and *spoil.*

Assessment *(AF 1)* Can the children sound talk and spell the *oi* words?

Objective Read phonically decodable two syllable words (5.7).

W Remind the children what 'syllable' means.

- Ask the children to show sound buttons for the word *Kipper.*
- Which sound is made by the *er*? (Its technical name is schwa.)
- Can children find other words in the book that end with *er?* (*silver, banner, corner, winner*)
- Talk about where *er* occurs in the words and confirm the sound it represents.

Assessment *(AF 1)* Can children identify where in a word schwa is represented by *er* ?

Objective To recognize the main events that shape different texts (7.3).

C *(Summarising)*

- Ask each child to look through the book and show the picture of what they think is the most important event in the story. Clarify that there isn't a right answer, so all opinions will be listened to.
- Discuss the different opinions. Model justifying your choice then give all children the opportunity to justify their own decisions as well as to challenge others.
- As a group, agree what the three main events are.

Assessment *(AF 4)* Can the children identify a key event and justify their choice of the event?

Speaking, listening and drama activities

Objective Listen to and follow instructions

C *(Clarifying)*

- **You will need:** some flat and 3D shapes including those representing the shapes needed to make the rocket: cylinder, cone, truncated cone, rectangles for fins. These can either be shapes or boxes for junk modelling.

- Let each child experiment by themselves, selecting the shapes they want to use to show their own version of the rocket. They shouldn't stick or join the shapes, just select them.
- Working in pairs, children give instructions to their partner in order to help them to build the rocket. The instruction–giver must not hold the shapes. The instruction receiver can ask questions to clarify the instructions, and should attempt to follow them as accurately as possible.
- If possible, let children record each stage of their rocket making with a digital camera.

Assessment *(AF 2)* Can the children both give and follow clear, step by step instructions?

Writing activities

Objective Convey information and ideas in simple non-narrative forms (9.3).

C *(Clarifying)*

- Ask children to write instructions for making a rocket.
- The instructions could either relate to the rocket in the book, or to the one they designed for the speaking and listening activity above.
- If digital photographs exist of the rocket making activity, they could be used to structure and sequence the instructions.

Assessment *(Writing AF 2)* Can the children create an appropriate text, independently?